Rabbity Cooking Six

Rabbity Cooking Six

CAROLINE MACLEOD

Rev. date: 05/04/2016

To order additional copies of this book, contact:
Xlibris
800-056-3182
www.Xlibrispublishing.co.uk
Orders@Xlibrispublishing.co.uk
741693

CONTENTS

SOLDIERS SIX FIGHTING

INTRODUCTION

THIS IS THE SECOND BOOK OF TWO THE FORMER BEING
CALLED TO LOOSE ALL PLUMS. THIS BOOK GIVES AN EASY
WAY TO COOK SIMPLY WITH A TALKATIVE MANNER USED
TO DESCRIBE THE GUIDES IN THIS BOOK. THERE ARE
MANY TIPS AND HINTS THAT ARE GIVEN SIMPLY.

FOREWORD

ABOUT COOKING WE ARE ALL GOING INTO A WORLD MORE ABOUT MONEY THAN HEALTH IN EATING. WE ARE BEING WORRIED SO MUCH ABOUT OUR WEIGHT THAN WE ARE BECOMING SCARED OF WALKING A ROUND. WE ALL DO STRUGGLE TO COPE SO A LITTLE BIT OF WHAT YOU FANCY DOES YOU GOOD.

SECTION 1

HAM

CLOVES – FOR DECORATING THE GLAZE

1 GAMMON JOINT

1 BAYLEAF

PEPPERCORNS – SEVERAL

DIJON MUSTARD

DEMARARA SUGAR

SOAK THE GAMMON IN WATER OVERNIGHT IN THE FRIDGE AND THEN DISCARD THE WATER.

PLACE PEPPERCORNS IN WATER AND ADD HAM. BRING TO A GENTLE SIMMER AND CONTINUE TO SIMMER FOR 1 ½ HOURS. THE WATER HAS TO COVER THE HAM. COOL IN THE WATER.

REMOVE FROM PAN AND SLICE OFF SKIN LEAVING ALL OF THE WHITE FAT UNDERNEATH THE SKIN, ON THE HAM.

CRISSCROSS THE MEAT IN A DIAMOND PATTERN ON THE FAT AND PUT A CLOVE IN EACH DIAMOND SHAPE. SPREAD THE DIJON MUSTARD ALL OVER THE FAT AND SPRINKLE THE SUGAR OVER PATTING IT DOWN ON THE SIDES. LEAVE THE MEAT BARE.

BAKE IN THE OVEN AT 220 CENTIGRADE UNTIL A CRUST IS FORMED WHICH TAKES ABOUT 12 – 15 MINUTES.

MARZIPAN

BUY YOUR MARZIPAN/ALMOND PASTE

PUT SOME APRICOT GLAZE, WARMED FIRST, ON TO THE CAKE JUST BEFORE ROLLING OUT THE MARZIPAN TO A ½ CENTIMETER THICKNESS AND ROUGHLY COVERING THE TOP OF THE CAKE.

THEN AFTER 2 HOURS UNCOVERED – TO LET IT SET AND DRY OUT SLIGHTLY – YOU CAN PUT THE ICING ON TOP.

WHITE ROYAL GLACE ICING

1 EGG WHITE

1 TEASPOON GLYCERINE

1 KILOGRAM OF ICING SUGAR

1 TEASPOON ROSE WATER

PUT THE EGG WHITES, GLYCERINE AND WATER IN TO A MIXING BOWL AND ADD ICING SUGAR UNTIL THERE IS A VERY STIFF MIXTURE THAT IS TOO HARD TO MIX. SPOON ON TO CAKE AND ROUGHLY FORK IT TO MAKE A SNOW SCENE.

MINCE PIES

2 PACKETS OF READY ROLL SHORTCRUST PASTRY

2 FLUID OUNCES OF RUM

1 GOOD BOTTLE OF MINCEMEAT

1 EGG BEATEN

2 OZ OF CASTER SUGAR

ROLL OUT PASTRY TO ½ CENTIMETER THICKNESS AND ADD THE RUM TO THE MINCEMEAT. MAKE UP THE MINCE PIES BY NOT PUTTING TOO MUCH FILLING IN. THAT WAY YOU CAN EAT MORE OF THEM.

SEAL AND COVER THEM WITH EGG WASH AND COVER WITH A SPRINKLING OF SUGAR.

BAKE AT 220 CENTIGRADE FOR 15 – 20 MINUTES.

RUM TRIFLE

RUM ½ BOTTLE

2 PACKETS OF TRIFLE CAKES OR SPONGE FINGERS

2 CARTONS OF STRAWBERRIES OR FROZEN RASPBERRIES

½ PINT FRESHLY SQUEEZED ORANGE JUICE

½ PINT SUGAR SYRUP MADE FROM BOILING ¾ PINT OF WATER WITH 10 OUNCES OF GRANULATED SUGAR FOR 8 MINUTES.

CUSTARD

CREAM

FLAKED CHOCOLATE

PUT TRIFLE CAKES IN BOTTOM OF PUDDING BASIN AND POUR OVER SYRUP, RUM, ORANGE AND STRAWBERRIES SLICED.

POUR OVER CUSTARD AND LEAVE FOR A COUPLE OF HOURS.

WHISK CREAM UNTIL SOFT THICK PEAKS FORM AND PLACE ON TOP OF CUSTARD ON TRIFLE.

DECORATE WITH STRAWBERRIES AND FLAKED CHOCOLATE.

CHOCOLATE FUDGE CHEESECAKE

1 PACKET OF TOFFEE

1 PINT OF DOUBLE CREAM

¾ PACK OF BUTTER

1 LARGE BAR OF BOURNVILLE CHOCOLATE WHICH IS 200 GRAMMES

MELT TOGETHER THE ABOVE INGREDIENTS ON A MEDIUM HEAT OR PUT IN TO THE MICROWAVE ON HIGH FOR 1 MINUTE AT A TIME UNTIL THE CHOCOLATE IS MELTING.

ADD TO 1 PACKET OF PHILADELPHIA CREAM CHEESE AND 4 EGGS AND 6 OUNCES OF SELF-RAISING FLOUR.

POUR INTO A BAKED BLIND PASTRY CASE AND BAKE IN THE OVEN AT 150 DEGREES CENTIGRADE FOR 45 MINUTES OR UNTIL SET IN THE CENTRE.

FRIED STEAK WITH MUSHROOM SAUCE

½ INCH THICK RUMP STEAK

FLOUR

SALT AND PEPPER

WILD PORCINI MUSHROOMS

CREAM

BEEF STOCK

PUT THE FLOUR ONTO A PLATE AND ADD A GENEROUS AMOUNT OF SALT AND PEPPER.

RUBB THE STEAK INTO THIS FLOUR MIXTURE.

FRY ON A GRIDDLE WITH A LITTLE HOT OIL ON HIGH HEAT FOR 3 MINUTES ON EACH SIDE TURNING FREQUENTLY AND THEN A FURTHER 3 MINUTES ON EACH SIDE ON MEDIUM HEAT.

PUT THE MUSHROOMS INTO 10 FLUID OUNCES OF BEEF STOCK AND BRING TO THE BOIL FOR FIVE MINUTES AND THEN ADD ½ PINT OF CREAM AND BOIL FOR 10 MINUTES TO REDUCE THE SAUCE. ADD SALT AND PEPPER AND SERVE WITH BAKED POTATOES AND BROCOLLI.

TURKEY FRICASSE

ALL THE LEFT OVER WHITE MEAT

ALL THE LEFT OVER DARK MEAT

GET YOUR FAVOURITE BBQ SAUCE AND MIX WITH THE DARK MEAT AND BAKE IN THE OVEN AT 200 CENTIGRADE FOR 20 – 25 MINUTES.

MAKE A WHITE SAUCE AND COOK THE WHITE MEAT IN IT FOR SEVERAL MINUTES.

SERVE WITH MASHED POTATOES AND SWEETCORN.

SCRAMBLED EGGS

ROUGHLY SPEAKING YOU WILL NEED 2 – 3 EGGS PER PERSON

A LITTLE SALT AND QUITE A LOT OF BLACK PEPPER

SOME BUTTER MELTED IN A SAUCEPAN

TAKE THE BUTTER IN THE SAUCEPAN AND ADD THE SALT AND PEPPER. HEAT UNTIL THE BUTTER IS FOAMING AND THEN CRACK IN THE EGGS. MIX WITH A WOODEN SPOON QUITE QUICKLY OVER A BRISK HEAT, UNTIL SOFT. TAKE OFF HEAT AND SERVE IMMEDIATELY WITH HOT BUTTERED TOAST.

DROP SCONES

1 EGG

2 ½ OUNCES OF PLAIN FLOUR

1 OUNCE OF GRANULATED WHITE SUGAR

A HANDFULL OF SULTANAS

5 FLUID OUNCES OF SOUR CREAM

1 TEASPOON OF BAKING POWDER

A LITTLE MILK

MIX ALL THE INGREDIENTS TOGETHER AND BEAT WITH A WHISK, THE RESULTING MIXTURE SHOULD BE A CREAMY TEXTURE AND HOLD THE BACK OF A SPOON, WHEN IT IS DIPPED IN IT.

HEAT A LITTLE BUTTER AND VEGETABLE OIL IN A FRYING PAN AND WHEN IT IS SIZZLING, ADD TEASPOONFULLS OF THE MIXTURE SEPARATELY ONTO THE PAN. COOK UNTIL BROWN ON BOTH SIDES AND ENJOY WHILE STILL WARM AND WITH BUTTER AND STRAWBERRY JAM.

MERINGUE ROLL

WHY NOT MAKE A MERINGUE AND THEN PUT IT IN A LARGE SWISS ROLL TIN OR OBLONG ON A LARGE FLAT BAKING SHEET ON A PIECE OF NON-STICK SILICONE BAKING SHEET AND COOK AT 150 CENTIGRADE FOR 50 MINUTES. THEN WHIP SOME CREAM AND SPREAD ON TOP, ONCE THE MERINGUE IS COOL, ADD SOME RASPBERRIES AND PUT A TABLESPOON OF GRAND MARNIER IN THE CREAM WITH A TABLESPOON OF ICING SUGAR BEFORE WHIPPING. WELL IT'S GOOD FOR A DIFFERENCE IF YOU'VE GOT NO CHILDREN EATING IT.

THEN ROLL IT UP USING THE SILICONE PAPER AND SCRAPING THE MERINGUE BACK FROM IT, AS YOU ROLL IT. DUST WITH ICING SUGAR.

IT'S A REALLY NICE DIFFERENCE TO HAVING A STRAIGHT PAVLOVA.

ASPARAGUS WITH HOLLANDAISE SAUCE

YOU ONLY NEED TO CUT OFF THE VERY THICK WOODY STEMS FROM THE ASPARAGUS. USUALLY ONLY AN INCH (3 CENTIMETERS) OR SO FROM THE SHOP BOUGHT ONES. LEAVE THE BUMPY ENDS TO EAT. THEY ARE THE BEST BIT OF IT.

BIG PAN OF BOILING WATER, SALTED AS IF FOR ORDINARY VEGETABLES. BOIL FOR 7 MINUTES. SHOULD BE TENDER IN MAIN BRANCH OF THE ASPARAGUS WITH A NORMAL EATING KNIFE.

SERVE WITH SOME WARMED HOLLANDAISE SAUCE YOU HAVE BOUGHT FROM THE SUPERMARKET OR MAKE YOU OWN AS DESCRIBED IN THIS BOOK LATER ON.

HALIBUT WITH ONION SAUCE

GET A THICK STEAK OF HALIBUT, ONE PER PERSON. SLICE A LARGE WHITE ONION IN THIS INSTANCE FOR TWO PEOPLE.

COOK IN VEGETABLE OIL ON A MEDIUM HEAT UNTIL CLEAR AND SOFT. ADD A SEASONING AND DESSERTSPOON OF SUGAR AND CARAMELISE WHICH MEAN COOKING ON FOR A FEW MINUTES. ADD SOME CHOPPED PARSLEY, A DROP OF LEMON JUICE AND HALF A PINT OF DOUBLE CREAM AND WARM THROUGH.

FRY THE HALIBUT ON BOTH SIDES ON GENTLE TO MEDIUM HEAT FOR ABOUT 6 MINUTES EACH SIDE. IF YOU ARE NOT SURE WHETHER IT IS COOKED THROUGH THEN TAKE AN EATING KNIFE AND CUT SOME ASIDE TO BE CERTAIN AS TO WHETHER IT IS.

SERVE WITH THE SAUCE POURED OVER IT AND WITH YOUR FAVOURITE BUTTERED AND SEASONED PEAS AND SOME NEW POTATOES, COOKED WITHOUT SALT AND SEASONED WITH MELTED BUTTER AND SALT AND PEPPER.

APPLE FOOL

YOU WILL NEED 2 COOKING APPLES

COOK SOME CHOPPED, PEELED AND DE-CORED COOKING APPLES WITH 150 GRAMMES OF GRANULATED WHITE SUGAR AND A DROP OF WATER WITH THE LID ON THE PAN OVER A HIGH HEAT. COOK THEM DOWN TO A PUREE AND LEAVE TO COOL.

WHIP ONE PINT OF DOUBLE CREAM UNTIL IT IS STIFF ENOUGH AND FALLS OFF THE BACK OF A SPOON WITH THE SLEIGHT OF A HAND. ADD 2 TABLESPOONS OF APPLE PUREE AT A TIME SO AS NOT TO LOOSEN THE CREAM TOO MUCH AND FOLD IN GENTLY. FOOL SHOULD BE THICK AND TASTY BUT RATHER THICK THAN TASTY. CREAM IS VERY FICKLE AND SHOULD BE TREATED WITH CARE.

ARMENIAN LAMB

YOU WILL NEED A HALF A SHOULDER OF LAMB FROM YOUR BUTCHER, CHOPPING IT IN TO 2 INCH PIECES, LEAVING ON THE FAT AND REMOVING THE BONE.

SLICE LARGE WHITE ONION AND COOK IN CASSEROLE DISH OR PAN ON TOP OF STOVE IN VEGETABLE OIL. ADD A TABLESPOON OF SUGAR AND CARAMELISE FOR A FEW MORE SECONDS. MEANWHILE FLOUR WITH SALT AND PEPPER THE PIECES OF LAMB AND ADD TO THE ONIONS ON A MEDIUM HEAT ADDING A TOUCH MORE VEGETABLE OIL IF NECESSARY, THEN ADD THE JUICE OF A FRESH ORANGE, A CAN OF CHOPPED TOMATOES AND A CAN OF DRAINED WASHED CHICKPEAS AND JUST COVER THE MEAT IN THE PAN WITH WATER.

PUT IN THE OVEN AT 180 CENTIGRADE FOR 2 ½ HOURS. SERVE WITH MASHED POTATOES.

RHUBARB SPONGE

2 CANS RHUBARB FROM THE SUPERMARKET ONE DRAINED OF SYRUP

HALF A SMALL PACKET OF BROWN SUGAR

1 PACKET OF BUTTER 250 GRAMMES

200 GRAMMES OF SELF-RAISING FLOUR

MAKE A BROWN SUGAR, BUTTER AND SELF-RAISING FLOUR CRUMBLE UNTIL QUITE WELL WORKED TOGETHER LOOKING LIKE THE BREADCRUMBS COULD TURN INTO PASTRY ANY SECOND WITHOUT ADDING ANYTHING. PUT ON TOP OF FRUIT IN PIE DISH AND COOK IN THE OVEN AT 180 CENTIGRADE FOR 45 MINUTES OR UNTIL THE TOP IS GOLDEN BROWN.

SERVE WITH HOMEMADE CUSTARD OR ONE FROM THE SUPERMARKET.

BEEF WITH ASPARAGUS

4 OUNCES OF FILLET STEAK CUT INTO VERY THIN STRIPS SO THAT YOU CAN NEARLY SEE THROUGH THEM.

LEAVE THE BOBBLY BITS ON THE ASPARAGUS AS THESE ARE THE PARTS YOU EAT AND CUT OFF THE LONG STALKS LEAVING ABOUT 3 INCHES LENGTH. STEAM THEM FOR 10 MINUTES.

FRY THE FILLET STEAK ON A GRIDDLE OVER VERY HOT HEAT, BURNING THEM SLIGHTLY.

MIX MELTED BUTTER AND LIGHT OLIVE OIL WITH BLACK PEPPER AND LEMON JUICE. ADD SOME SALT. POUR OVER THE ASPARAGUS AND FILLET STEAK AND SERVE ON A PLATE OF MIXED SALAD.

POTATOES PIE

CHOP SOME POTATOES AND FRY IN BUTTER IN THICK CHUNKS AFTER HAVING BOILED THEM FOR 5 MINUTES.

LINE A FLAN DISH WITH PASTRY AND PUT SOME STRONG CHEESE IN THE BOTTOM, PILE ON THE POTATOES AND ADD SOME MORE CHEESE AND POUR OVER ¼ PINT OF DOUBLE CREAM AND COVER WITH PASTRY. BRUSH TOP WITH EGG YOLK AND SALT AND BAKE AT 200 CENTIGRADE UNTIL THE PASTRY IS COOKED WHICH IS ABOUT 40 MINUTES.

SECTION 2

BEEF STEW WITH CARAMELISED ONIONS AND SAUTED MUSHROOMS

YOU WILL NEED SOME BRAISING STEAK CUT INTO LARGE CUBES

LARGELY CUT UP SOME CARROTS AND SMALLER CHOPPED ONIONS AND FOR THE END OF THE STEW YOU WILL NEED SOME EXTRA BUTTON ONIONS AND MUSHROOMS COOKED IN BUTTER AND THEN FURTHER COOKED WITH SUGAR FOR A FEW MINUTES TO CARAMELISE THEM.

STEW: PUT CARROTS AND CHOPPED ONIONS IN SOME VEGETABLE OIL IN A DEEP PAN AND SAUTE THEM. THEN ADD FLOURED, SALTED AND PEPPERED BRAISING STEAK PIECES AND FRY IN EXTRA VEGETABLE OIL UNTIL BROWN ON A MEDIUM TO HIGH HEAT. ADD WATER TO JUST COVER THE MEAT AND COOK AT 180 CENTIGRADE FOR 3 ½ HOURS. YOU WILL HAVE TO CHECK THE STEW CONSTANTLY BUT IT IS WELL WORTH COOKING IT ON THE TOP OF THE HOB AND KEEP ON STIRRING.

ADD THE CARAMELISED ONIONS AND MUSHROOMS JUST BEFORE SERVING. ALLOW THE MUSHROOMS AND ONIONS TO HEAT THROUGH IN THE STEW AND SERVE WITH MASHED POTATOES.

APPLE CRUMBLE

FOUR COOKING APPLES

SUGAR – 4 TABLESPOONS

FLOUR – PLAIN 200 GRAMMES

BUTTER – 1 PACKET 250 GRAMMES

MORE SUGAR FOR CRUMBLE TOPPING 150 GRAMMES

PEEL AND SLICE AND DE-CORE APPLES AND PUT IN OVENPROOF BOWL WITH 4 TABLESPOONS OF GRANULATED SUGAR AND A LITTLE WATER.

ADD A SPRINKLING OF CINNAMON, IF YOU LIKE IT.

TO MAKE THE CRUMBLE USE HARD BUTTER AND WORK IT IN TO THE FLOUR AND SUGAR MIXTURE WITH YOUR FINGERS OR YOU CAN USE A KNIFE.

WHEN IT RESEMBLES STICKY BREADCRUMBS, PUT IT ON TOP OF THE APPLES AND COOK FOR ¾ OF AN HOUR AT 170 CENTIGRADE OR UNTIL THE TOPPING HAS TURNED DARK GOLDEN BROWN.

SERVE WITH CUSTARD.

QUEEN'S PUDDING

MAKE AN EGG CUSTARD BY TAKING 6 EGG YOLKS AND ADDING 2 TEASPOONS OF CORNFLOUR AND MIXING THOROUGHLY. ADD 6 OUNCES OF CASTER SUGAR INTO A PINT OF CREAM AND HEAT UNTIL WARM AND ADD 2 FLUID OUNCES OF COINTREAU ORANGE LIQUEUR. POUR ONTO THE EGG YOLKS MIXING QUICKLY AND RETURN TO THE SAUCEPAN AND OVER GENTLE HEAT BRING TO JUST BEFORE SIMMERING POINT.

POUR THIS CUSTARD ON TOP OF THE HALVED PEACHES AND THROW IN A HANDFULL OF HAZELNUTS SCATTERING THEM ALL OVER THE PEACHES AND CUSTARD.

SET THE CUSTARD IN A BAIN-MARIE WHICH IS A DEEP PAN FILLED TO ONE THIRD THE HEIGHT OF THE PUDDING DISH IN AN OVEN AT 170 CENTIGRADE FOR 40 MINUTES.

WHILE IT IS COOKING BEAT THE EGG WHITES UNTIL FIRM AND ADD 6 OUNCES OF CASTER SUGAR AND KEEP HEATING UNTIL THE MIXTURE IS GLOSSY.

ADD ON TOP OF THE PEACHES AND CUSTARD AND BAKE FOR A FURTHER 35 MINUTES IN THE BAIN-MARIE.

CREME ANGLAISE TART WITH STRAWBERRIES AND RED GLAZE

FIRSTLY TAKE 1 PINT OF MILK AND WARM. PUT 4 EGG YOLKS IN TO A MIXING BOWL WITH A FEW DROPS OF VANILLA ESSENCE AND 5 OUNCES OF GRANULATED SUGAR AND 1 DESSERTSPOON OF PLAIN FLOUR AND MIX TOGETHER WITH A DROP OF COOL MILK. THEN TAKE THE WARM MILK AND WHILE MIXING POUR IT INTO THE YOLKS, THIS DONE QUICKLY MEANS THAT THE YOLK DISSIPATE AND THEREFORE DO NOT CURDLE. BRING TO JUST BELOW SIMMERING POINT AND THEN IMMEDIATELY TAKE OFF THE HEAT OTHERWISE THE EGGS WILL COOK AND CURDLE. THEN LEAVE TO COOL STIRRING FOR A LITTLE WHILE TO MAKE SURE THE CUSTARD DOESN'T CATCH ON THE BOTTOM OF THE PAN BUT DO NOT OVERSTIR OTHERWISE THE CUSTARD WILL GO RUNNY AGAIN. WHEN THE CUSTARD IS COLD WHIP UP HALF A PINT OF DOUBLE CREAM AND FOLD IT INTO THE CUSTARD.

MEANWHILE ROLL OUT A PACKET OF SHORTCRUST PASTRY AND LINE SOME SMALL TINS AND BAKE BLIND IN THE OVEN. THAT MEANS TO PUT A GREASEPROOF LINING ON TOP OF THE PASTRY AND FILL WITH DRIED BEANS BEFORE COOKING. COOK AT 200 CENTIGRADE FOR 20 MINUTES TO COOK THROUGH ENTIRELY.

WHEN THE PASTRY IS COOL, FILL IT WITH THE CREME ANGLAISE AND THEN HAVING WASHED A PACKET OF STRAWBERRIES AND CUT THEM INTO SMALL PIECES, SCATTER THEM ON TOP AND COVER WITH THE STRAWBERRY GELLO GLAZE THAT YOU CAN BUY IN A SUPERMARKET.

ROASTED RED PEPPERS

CHOP SOME RED PEPPERS IN HALF WITH THE STALK CUT THROUGH THE MIDDLE AND POP INTO A ROASTING TIN WITH CHOPPED FENNEL AND BUFFALO MOZZARELLA SLICED INTO THICK SLICES AND RE-HYDRATED WILD MUSHROOMS. SPRINKLE WITH OLIVE OIL AND SEASON WITH GARLIC PIECES AND SALT AND PEPPER. BAKE IN THE OVEN AT 200 CENTIGRADE 45 MINUTES. SERVE WITH FRENCH BREAD.

PAELLA WITH PANCETTA

GET SOME RISOTTO RICE AND PUT IT IN A PAN WITH SOME CHOPPED ONION AND SOME OLIVE OIL AND 2 CHOPPED RED CHILLI PEPPERS KEEPINGIN THE SEEDS. AFTER FRYING FOR 3 MINUTES ADD SOME BOILING WATER AND SOME HAM STOCK. ADD THE WILD MUSHROOMS WHICH HAVE BEEN RE-HYDRATED ACCORDING TO THE INSTRUCTIONS ON THE PACKET AND COOK WITH THE RICE UNTIL THE WATER HAS BEEN ABSORBED, ADDING MORE WATER UNTIL THE RICE HAS ALDENTE COOKED AND IS STILL SOUPY. ADD THE PANCETTA, PEAS, THE GOAT'S CHEESE AND SOME FRESH MARJORAM. SEASON WITH SALT AND PEPPER AND SERVE WITH SOME GREEN SALAD.

RASPBERRY FILO PASTRY WITH CREAM AND CUSTARD SAUCE

GET A PACKET OF FILO PASTRY FROM THE SUPERMARKET AND PLACE 4 SHEETS ON TOP OF EACH OTHER WITH MELTED BUTTER BRUSHED ON EACH SHEET ALL OVER. PUT MELTED BUTTER ALL OVER THE TOP SHEET TOO. MAKE HOLES WITH A SHARP FORK ALL OVER THE FILO PASTRY AND THEN TAKE A SMALL TART CUTTER, ABOUT 3 INCHES ACROSS AND CUT OUT 12 ROUNDS FOR 4 PEOPLE.

BAKE THEM IN THE OVEN AT 200 CENTIGRADE FOR ABOUT 15 MINUTES. LEAVE TO COOL.

WHIP 1 PINT OF DOUBLE CREAM WITH 1 OUNCE OF ICING SUGAR AND 1 SHOT OF GRAND MARNIER.

GET SOME CUSTARD FROM THE SUPERMARKET, SOME OF THEIR BEST IS REALLY SOMETIMES, UNBEATABLE.

PUT A DOT OF CREAM ON THE PUDDING PLATE FOR EACH PERSON, PLACE ON TOP A ROUND OF COOKED PASTRY, PLACING ON TOP A DESSERTSPOON OF CREAM, THEN A FEW RASPBERRIES, FROZEN IF YOU PREFER, BUT MAKE SURE YOU SWEETEN THEM WITH A LITTLE CASTER SUGAR AND WARM THEM FOR SEVERAL SECONDS TO DISSOLVE THE SUGAR. THEN PLACE A SMALL SPOONFULL OF CUSTARD ON TOP OF THE RASPBERRIES, AND PLACE A PASTRY PIECE ON TOP OF THAT. ONCE YOU HAVE MADE THEM ALL, SPRINKLE EACH WITH ICING SUGAR, IT DOESN'T MATTER IF SOM EGOES ON THE PLATE, AND SERVE.

CHICKEN WITH CURRIED CREAM AND SULTANAS

YOU NEED ONE CHICKEN BREAST PER PERSON AND YOU NEED TO ADD SOME VEGETABLE OIL TO A DEEP FRYING PAN AND ADD THE CHICKEN BREASTS, CHOPPED IF YOU PREFER – AND THEN COOK THEM OVER A GENTLE TO MEDIUM HEAT UNTIL THEY ARE HALF COOKED. THEN ADD 2 CHOPPED ONIONS AND 1 TABLESPOON OF HOT MADRAS CURRY PASTE AND CONTINUE COOKING FOR TWO MINUTES UNTIL THE CURRY PASTE HAS COOKED THROUGH AND THEN ADD 2 HANDFULLS OF SULTANAS AND 1 PINT OF DOUBLE POURING CREAM. ADD A BANANA ROUGHLY CHOPPED IF YOU LIKE. ALLOW THE SAUCE TO COOK ON GENTLE HEAT UNTIL THE CREAM HAS GONE INTO THE SAUCE AND THE CHICKEN IS FIRMLY COOKED. SERVE WITH CHIPS.

HAM AND SPLIT YELLOW PEA SOUP

TWO ONIONS

2 HANDFULLS OF YELLOW SPLIT PEAS

1 POTATO

2 CARROTS

1 LEEK

1 SWEDE/TURNIP

1 HAM JOINT

PUT SOME VEGETABLE OIL INTO A PAN AND ADD THE CHOPPED ONIONS, CARROTS, LEEK, TURNIP, POTATO AND YELLOW SPLIT PEAS AND SOME BLACK PEPPERCORNS. COOK IN THE OIL UNTIL THEY HAVE SOFTENED SLIGHTLY. ADD 3 PINTS OF WATER AND THE HAM JOINT AND BRING TO THE BOIL. COOK UNTIL THE PEAS HAVE TOTALLY COOKED DOWN.

TAKE OUT THE HAM AND SERVE AFTER THE SOUP, WITH POTATO DAUPHINOISE WHICH IS POTATOES SLICED THEN BAKED WITH HALF FAT CREME FRAICHE AND MUSTARD MIXED IN. DON'T FORGET TO SEASON IT. COOK THE POTATOES AT 200 CENTIGRADE FOR 1 HOUR.

ROAST VENISON

4/5 POUND JOINT OF VENISON

SALT AND PEPPER

OIL

STOCK

WITH THE BONE THE JOINT WILL TAKE AN EXTRA HALF AN HOUR.

PUT THE VENISON JOINT IN A ROASTING TIN AND SEASON WITH SALT AND PEPPER AND ADD 1 PINT OF LAMB STOCK. COVER THE JOINT AND TIGHTEN TO THE SIDES OF THE ROASTING TIN SOME SILVER FOIL AND ROAST THE VENISON FOR 2 HOURS AT 220 CENTIGRADE.

SERVE WITH CAULIFLOWER CHEESE AND REDCURRANT JELLY AND ROAST POTATOES AND GRAVY.

HOLLANDAISE

2 PACKETS OF BUTTER

2 FLUID OUNCES OF WHITE WINE VINEGAR

6 EGG YOLKS

8 BLACK PEPPERCORNS

A LITTLE SALT TO TASTE

1 TEASPOON CUMIN

OVER A DOUBLE SAUCEPAN PUT IN PEPPERCORNS, VINEGAR AND CUMIN AND BOIL RAPIDLY FOR 1 MINUTE.

TAKE THE SAUCEPAN OFF THE HEAT AND LET THE REMAINING LIQUID COOL, SLIGHTLY AND LET THE PAN GO COOL. ADD ALL OF THE EGG YOLKS AT ONCE, AT THE SAME TIME AS A BIT OF THE SOFTENED BUTTER, WHISKING CONTINUOUSLY, RETURNING THE SAUCEPAN TO THE DOUBLE SAUCEPAN ON THE HEAT STILL. THE WATER IN THE DOUBLE SAUCEPAN SHOULD BE SIMMERING RAPIDLY. CONTINUE ADDING THE PIECES OF BUTTER TO THE MIXTURE RAPIDLY WHILST STILL WHISKING RAPIDLY. THE MIXTURE SHOULD START TO THICKEN.

CONTINUE TO ADD ALL THE BUTTER IN BITS, WHISKING CONTINUOUSLY AND THEN TAKE THE SAUCEPAN OFF THE HEAT IMMEDIATELY THAT THE SAUCE HAS THICKENED. DO NOT RE-HEAT.

DON'T WORRY IF IT IS STILL A BIT RUNNY, IT WILL STILL TASTE NICE.

BE CAREFULL NOT TO LET THE SAUCE IN THE TOP SAUCEPAN GET TOO HOT OR IT WILL COOK THE EGG YOLKS AND CURDLE.

FOR BEARNAISE JUST ADD SOME TARRAGON IN THE BUTTER STAGE.

"RED" VEAL ESCALOPES

I ALWAYS USE CALVES THAT HAVE BEEN FED IN THE FIELD
FOR AN APPROX. YEAR.

ESCALOPES OF VEAL

FLOUR

SALT AND PEPPER

COOK ONE AFTER THE OTHER.

FRY FOR 3 MINUTES ON BOTH SIDES ON A MEDIUM HEAT.

SERVE WITH ASPARAGUS STEAMED FOR 8 MINUTES WITH
HOLLANDAISE ON THE SIDE.

PUNCH

3 BOTTLES WHITE WINE

1 BOTTLE ROSE CHEAP SWEET

SPARKLING WINE

LOTS OF FRUIT TO EAT

SERVE IN FLAT GLASSES AND MAKE SURE THE GLASSES ARE FULL OF FRUIT AND YOU HAVE A SPOON TO EAT IT WITH.

SQUASH SALAD

TOMATOES OLIVES MARJORAM OLIVE OIL BALSAMIC VINEGAR MOZARELLA CHEESE AND LEMON AND ASPARAGUS AND WARM FRIED BOILED SQUASHES.

CHOP THEM ALL UP TO LOOK ATTRACTIVE, SPRINKLE OVER THE CHEESE AND SERVE WITH THE OIL AND BALSAMIC VINEGAR DRIZZLED OVER THE TOP. PEEL THE LEMON AND GET THE SEGMENTS AND ADD TO THE SALAD AT THE LAST MINUTE.

SMOKED SALMON AND GREEN PEA PASTA

CHILLIES

OLIVE OIL

SMOKED SALMON

SHALLOTS

PASTA SHELLS – COOKED AND COLD

GREEN PEAS – COOKED AND WARM

CHIVES

CHOP THE CHILLIES FINELY AND ALSO THE SHALLOTS. TEAR UP THE SMOKED SALMON AND CHOP THE CHIVES AND MIX EVERYTHING TOGETHER AND LEAVE TO REST FOR AN HOUR. SEASON WITH PEPPER AND A LITTLE SALT.

"RED" VEAL MINCE WITH PASTA

MACARONI LAYERED WITH:

MEAT SAUCE WITH CAPERS AND LEMONS, TOMATOES, A PINCH OF BROWN SUGAR OR A SPOON OF TREACLE AND SOME OUZO/PASTIS AND CHIVES.

CHEESE AND EGG SAUCE WITH RICOTTA AND MARSCAPONE GOES ON ONE LAYER IN MIDDLE AND ONE LAYER ON TOP.

PASTA WITH WHITE FISH SAUCE

FISH STOCK ½ PINT

SINGLE CREAM ½ PINT

PINCH PARSLEY FLAT LEAF

LEMON ½ GENTLY SQUEEZED

PEAS

PINCH CORIANDER LEAVES

SPAGHETTI/VERMICELLI

GRATED MOZARELLA

BOIL TOGETHER THE FISH STOCK AND THE CREAM AND COOK SEPARATELY THE PEAS AND WHEN COOKED ADD THE PEAS TO THE SAUCE AND THE RIPPED HERBS. COOK THE PASTA AND ADD THE LEMON AND THE SAUCE AND MIX WELL. SEASON TO TASTE AND SERVE WITH THE MOZARELLA.

CHICKEN AND WHITEBAIT SALAD

CHICKEN BREASTS

GARLIC

OLIVE OIL

RED CHILLI

WHITE BAIT

CRISP LETTUCE SALAD – ROMAINE/LITTLEGEM

LEMON LIGHTLY SQUEEZED

CUT CHICKEN BREAST THINLY ACROSS THE WAY AND FRY IN OLIVE OIL AND FRY FLOURED WHITEBAIT AND ADD TO CHOPPED GARLIC AND CHILLI AND CRISP GREEN SALAD SPRINKLED WITH LEMON AND SEASONED.

SALMON STICKS

CUT A SALMON FILLET INTO THIN STRIPS AND FRY ON HIGH HEAT IN OLIVE OIL, SALT AND PEPPER.

PLACE OVER A SAVARIN MOULDED RICE WHICH HAS BEEN FRIED WITH TUMERIC AND CHOPPED SHALLOTS BEFORE BOILING. SEASON.

SERVE TEPID.

ICECREAM AND TOFFEE SURPRISE

SOME VANILLA SOFT SCOOP: YOU CAN MAKE THIS WITH CUSTARD AND 2 TEASPOONS OF VANILLA ESSENCE AND 1 PINT OF DOUBLE CREAM WHICH IS THEN FROZEN.

MELT TOGETHER 1 PACKET OF TOFFEE WITH 1 CAN OF CONDENSED MILK AND ADD SOME MAPLE SYRUP. FREEZE UNTIL STIFF WHICH IS ABOUT 2/3 HOURS.

LOOSLEY FOLD TOGETHER AND SERVE.

ROCK CAKES

1 OUNCE OF DESSICATED COCONUT

1 TEASPOON ALMOND ESSENCE

1 OUNCE OF PLAIN FLOUR

1 OUNCE OF GROUND ALMONDS

2 OUNCES OF GRANULATED SUGAR

1 OUNCE OF CURRANTS

5 OUNCES OF BUTTER

MIX DRY INGREDIENTS TOGETHER AND RUBB IN BUTTER THEN ADD SOME WATER TO COMBINE. FORM INTO ROCK PEAKS AND BAKE IN AN OVEN FOR 14 MINUTES AT 180 CENTIGRADE. THEY SHOULD BE LARVA – ROCK. I WAS TOLD THAT IN MY CHILDHOOD.

SOLDIERS SIX
FIGHTING

FOR LE REPAS AND DINNER PARTIES

TO HAVE A FEW OF YOUR FAVOURITE DIGESTIVES AT THE
END OR THE BEGINNING OF YOUR MEAL IS GOOD.

MENU 1

TOASTED GOATS CHEESE

BEEF WELLINGTON

RASPBERRY MERINGUE

TOASTED GOATS CHEESE

INDIVIDUAL GOATS CHEESES

BASIL

LEMON THYME

OREGANO

BLACK PEPPER

OLIVE OIL

CUT THE GOATS CHEESES IN HALF HORIZONTALLY AND SPRINKLE ON HERBS AND BLACK PEPPER ON THE CUT SIDE OF THE GOATS CHEESES.

DRIZZLE OVER A TABLESPOON OF OLIVE OIL AND GRILL UNDER A MODERATE TO HOT GRILL FOR 8 MINUTES OR UNTIL GOLDEN BROWN.

SERVE WITH SOME CRISPY GREEN SALAD AND CRUSTY BREAD.

Caroline Macleod

BEEF WELLINGTON

TAKE A FAT END FILLET OF BEEF AND SEASON WELL WITH SALT AND PEPPER. BROWN ON ALL SIDES ON A HOT GRIDDLE AND LEAVE TO COOL FOR 5 MINUTES.

TAKE SOME MUSHROOM PATE AND SPREAD IT ALL OVER THE FILLET.

GET 2 PACKETS OF PUFF PASTRY AND ROLL OUR TO HALF A CENTIMETER THICKNESS.

GET SOME BEATEN EGG WITH SALT READY.

PUT THE BEEF IN THE CENTRE OF THE ROLLED OUT PASTRY AND BRING THE SIDES UP TO THE TOP MAKING THE PASTRY ENCASEMENT OF THE FILLET COMPLETELY COVERED. IT MIGHT BE EASIER TO MAKE THE JOIN UNDERNEATH THE FILLET.

DECORATE WITH THE LEFT OVER PASTRY BY MAKING FLOWERS AND STICKING THEM ON TOP OF THE FILLET IN PASTRY WITH SOME OF THE EGG GLAZE.

GLAZE THE WHOLE PASTRY WITH EGG GLAZE AND ROAST IN THE OVEN AT 220 CENTIGRADE FOR 45 MINUTES.

CUT IN THICK SLICES AND SERVE WITH NEW POTATOES AND CARROTS AND SPRING CABBAGE TOSSED IN BUTTER WITH SALT AND BUTTER AND GRAVY.

YOU MAY NEED TO ADD A TABLESPOON OF OIL WITH THE BUTTER BEFORE BROWNING.

BEURRE NOISETTE

THIS IS THE GRAVY THAT GOES WITH A BEEF WELLINGTON.

WHEN MAKING BUERRE NOISETTE YOU HAVE TO BE VERY QUICK IN THE INITIAL STAGES. FIRST BROWN SOME BUTTER AND OIL AND AS SOON AS IT STARTS TO GO BROWN AND NUTTY ADD SOME FLOUR AND TOMATO PUREE AND THEN ADD SOME STOCK OF YOUR FAVOURITE TYPE EVEN FISH STOCK IS FAVOURITE TO SOME PEOPLE, AND WHISK IT TO SIMMERING POINT FOR A MINUTE AND THEN SEASON WITH SALT AND PEPPER. YOU CAN USE ANY OIL YOU LIKE, SOME PEOPLE USE WALNUT OIL.

RASPBERRY MERINGUE

WIPE OUT A MIXING BOWL AND BEATERS WITH VINEGAR TO CLEANSE THE GREASE AWAY. EGG WHITES ARE PARTICULARLY PRONE TO UNDER DEVELOPING WHEN WHISKED EVEN WHEN THE POTS USED ARE CLEAN.

4 ROOM TEMPERATURE EGGS

6 OUNCES OF CASTER SUGAR

WHISK EGG WHITES WITH AN ELECTRIC BEATER OR BY USING A HAND WHISK UNTIL THE WHITES ARE FORMING PEAKS. ADD A LITTLE SUGAR AT A TIME UNTIL IT IS ALL USED UP. KEEP ON WHISKING UNTIL THE EGG WHITES AND SUGAR ARE SHINEY AND WELL THICKENED INTO PEAKS.

PILE THE MERINGUE ON TO BAKING PARCHMENT IN A CIRCLE QUITE THICK AND BAKE AT 180 CENTIGRADE FOR 30 – 40 MINUTES.

LEAVE TO COOL.

TAKING IT OFF THE BAKING PARCHMENT MAY NEED 2 PALLET KNIVES.

WHIP ONE PINT OF DOUBLE CREAM WITH A LITTLE ICING SUGAR AND 1 FLUID OUNCE OF GRAND MARNIER UNTIL SOFT AND FLUFFY AND FORMING PEAKS. SPREAD ON TOP OF PAVLOVA AND COVER WITH RASPBERRIES AND DECORATE WITH MINT LEAVES.

MENU 2

ROASTED PEPPERS

LEMON SOLE

CHOCOLATE MOUSSE

ROASTED PEPPERS

CUT A RED PEPPER IN HALF THROUGH THE GREEN STALK KEEPING HALF THE STALK ON EACH SIDE. USE HALF A STALK FOR EACH PERSON. PLACE WITH THE CUT SIDE UP IN A ROASTING PAN AND DRIZZLE OVER OLIVE OIL AND PLACE SMALL SPRATS OVER THE TOP AND SEASON WITH SALT AND PEPPER.

ROAST THEM FOR ABOUT 40 MINUTES IN THE OVEN AT 200 CENTIGRADE. IT WILL MAKE QUITE A LOT OF JUICES WHICH SHOULD BE SERVED WITH THE PEPPERS AND MOPPED UP WITH CRUSTY BREAD.

LEMON SOLE

TAKE ONE FILLET OF SOLE PER PERSON AND DIP IT IN FLOUR. FRY QUICKLY IN A FRYING PAN WITH SOME VEGETABLE OIL AND SEASON WITH SALT AND PEPPER. SERVE WITH NEW POTATOES AND SOME GREEN BEANS COATED IN GARLIC BUTTER.

CHOCOLATE MOUSSE

WHISK HALF A PINT OF DOUBLE CREAM UNTIL SOFT PEAKS FORM. MELT 200 GRAMMES OF CHOCOLATE IN THE MICROWAVE ON FULL POWER FOR 1 MINUTE. WHISK 3 EGG WHITES AND THEN FOLD ALL THE INGREDIENTS TOGETHER. CHILL.

MENU 3

SPINACH EGGS FLORENTINE

TROUT IN HAM AND CREAM SAUCE

STRAWBERRY AND CREAM MILLE FEUILLE

SPINACH EGGS FLORENTINE

PUT SOME FROZEN SPINACH IN A SAUCEPAN WITH SOME BUTTER AND COOK IT OVER MEDIUM HEAT UNTIL IT IS ALL DEFROSTED. IT WILL DRY OUT AS IT COOKS. ADD A GRATING OF NUTMEG AND SOME SALT AND PEPPER. PUT A LAYER IN A RAMEKING DISH AND ADD A LAYER OF DOUBLE CREAM AND THEN AN EGG AND THEN SOME PARMESAN CHEESE ON TOP. BAKE AT 180 CENTIGRADE FOR 15 – 20 MINUTES AND SERVE WITH SOME BREAD AND BUTTER.

TROUT IN HAM AND CREAM SAUCE

CUT SOME THICK SLICED HAM INTO MATCHSTICKS. TAKE 1 FILLET OF TROUT PER PERSON AND FRY IN BUTTER SALT AND PEPPER AND CHOPPED PARSLEY FOR 1 MINUTE ON EACH SIDE. POUR IN ½ PINT OF DOUBLE CREAM AND PUT IN THE HAM AND SIMMER FOR 1 MINUTE. SERVE WITH RICE AND PEAS.

STRAWBERRY AND CREAM MILLE FEUILLE

ROLL OUT A PACKET OF PUFF PASTRY IN TO AN OBLONG SHAPE AND CUT 8 OBLONGS OUT OF IT. THE PASTRY SHOULD BE ½ A CENTIMETER THICK. PRICK 4 OF THEM ALL OVER WITH A FORK.

THE OTHER 4 SHOULD BE GLAZED WITH EGG YOLK AND SPRINKLED WITH CASTER SUGAR.

COOK ALL OF THE PASTRY SLICES AT 200 CENTIGRADE FOR 15 MINUTES OR UNTIL GOLDEN BROWN.

TAKE OUT OF THE OVEN AND LEAVE TO COOL COMPLETELY.

WHISK 1 OUNCE OF ICING SUGAR WITH HALF A PINT OF DOUBLE CREAM UNTIL IT HOLDS ITS WEIGHT WELL ENOUGH ON A SPOON. CHOP SOME STRAWBERRIES AND ADD SOME SUGAR AND LEAVE TO MACERATE FOR A WHILE. FOLD THE STRAWBERRIES IN TO THE CREAM LEAVING A BIT OF CREAM FOR HOLDING DOWN THE PASTRIES TO THE SERVING PLATE.

PLACE THE PRICKED PASTRY SLICES ON A SERVING PLATE PUTTING A DOT OF CREAM UNDERNEATH EACH ONE OF THEM TO HOLD THEM STEADY AND THEN PLACE THE FILLING ON TOP OF THEM ALL FOLLOWED BY THE GLAZED PASTRY SLICES. DUST THEM ALL WITH ICING SUGAR AND SERVE.

MENU 4

SEA BREAM

BOMBE GALORE

SEA BREAM

TAKE CARE TO CHECK THE SEA BREAM FILLETS FOR BONES. SIMMER 1 PINT OF DOUBLE CREAM WITH A FEW SPRIGS OF ROSEMARY AND BASIL AND SALT AND PEPPER. FRY THE SEA BREAM FILLETS FOR 4 – 5 MINUTES ON EACH SIDE AND ADD CREAM TO FRYING PAN AND LET IT HEAT THROUGH. SERVE WITH LINGUINI TOSSED WITH CHERRY TOMATOES THAT HAVE BEEN ROASTED IN THE OVEN WITH OLIVE OIL AND SALT AND PEPPER FOR 20 MINUTES AT 220 CENTIGRADE.

BOMBE GALORE

APRICOT COMPOTE

1 TUB OF PHILADELPHIA CREAM CHEESE

HALF A PINT OF DOUBLE CREAM

1 SHOT OF RUM

4 MERINGUE NESTS

MIX THE CREAM CHEESE WITH THE DOUBLE CREAM AND CAREFULLY FOLD IN THE RUM AND APRICOT COMPOTE AND BROKEN UP MERINGUE NESTS. PUT IN TO A PUDDING BOWL AND FREEZE OVERNIGHT. DIP IN HOT WATER TO TURN OUT AND DECORATE WITH FRUIT AND SERVE.

MENU 5

MUSSELS FLORENTINE

LEMON CREAM

MUSSELS FLORENTINE

DEFROST THE SPINACH IN A PAN OVER MEDIUM HEAT WITH BUTTER AND SALT AND PEPPER STIRRING REGULARLY.

PUT SOME WHITE WINE IN A PAN WITH A TIGHT FITTING LID AND PUT IN SOME MUSSELS WHICH HAVE HAD ALL OF THEIR HAIR PULLED OUT. PUT ON A HIGH HEAT AND LEAVE TO STEAM FOR 2 – 3 MINUTES AFTER THE STEAM HAS STARTED TO ESCAPE FROM THE PAN.

MAKE A CHEESE SAUCE.

WHEN THE MUSSELS HAVE OPENED IN THE PAN REMOVE FROM THE HEAT STRAIGHT AWAY AND REMOVE MUSSELS FROM THE PAN. TAKE THE MUSSELS OUT OF THE SHELLS AND TAKE CARE TO KEEP THE SHELLS.

PUT THE MUSSEL SHELL HALVES ON A BAKING SHEET AND FILL WITH SPINACH THEN PLACE ON TOP A MUSSEL AND THEN ON TOP OF THAT PUT SOME CHEESE SAUCE. SPRINKLE OVER SOME PARMESAN AND PLACE UNDER THE GRILL TO BROWN.

Caroline Macleod

LEMON CREAM

1 PINT OF DOUBLE CREAM

2 EGG WHITES

2 OUNCES OF CASTER SUGAR

2 LEMONS

WHIP THE DOUBLE CREAM WITH THE RUM AND WHISK THE EGG WHITES UNTIL THEY HAVE FORMED STIFF PEAKS ADDING THE SUGAR TO THE EGG WHITES ONCE THEY HAVE PEAKED AND CONTINUING TO WHISK. SQUEEZE THE JUICE OUT OF THE LEMONS AND ADD TO THE MERINGUE AND THEN FOLD IN THE DOUBLE CREAM AND RUM MIXTURE.

MENU 6

CHEESE SOUFFLE

SEA BASS ON RED CABBAGE

CHEESE SOUFFLE

MAKE A PINT OF VERY STRONG FLAVOURED CHEESE SAUCE AND ADD TO IT 3 EGG YOLKS WHILE IT IS NOT TOO HOT AND BEAT IN.

WHISK THE EGG WHITES UNTIL STIFF AND FOLD INTO THE CHEESE SAUCE.

PUT INTO A SOUFFLE DISH UNTIL HALFWAY UP THE SIDES AND PLACE IN AN OVEN AT 220 CENTIGRADE FOR 40 MINUTES.

SERVE WITH CRUSTY BREAD AND BUTTER FOR DIPPING.

SEA BASS ON RED CABBAGE

TAKE A FAVOURITE RED CABBAGE RECIPE AND MAKE IT OR USE RED CABBAGE ALREADY MADE UP FROM A SUPERMARKET.

YOU WILL NEED ONE FILLET OF SEA BASS PER PERSON.

PUT THE FILLETS OF SEA BASS IN TO INDIVIDUAL SILVER FOIL PARCELS AND ADD SOME WHITE WINE AND CREME FRAICHE AND A FEW PEPPERCORNS IN EACH ONE.

BAKE IN THE OVEN IN A ROASTING TIN AT 220 CENTIGRADE FOR 30 MINUTES.

SERVE WITH PEAS AND NEW POTATOES TURNED IN BUTTER AND SALT AND PEPPER AND GARLIC.

MENU 7

WATERCRESS BEETROOT AND BROCCOLI SALAD

SALMON AND PLAICE ROLL

FRESH FRUIT BRANDY

WATERCRESS BEETROOT AND BROCCOLI SALAD

THOROUGHLY WASH SOME WATERCRESS.

COOK SOME BROCCOLI CUT UP INTO TINY FLORETS UNTIL JUST ALDENTE.

COOK SOME FRESH BEETROOT BY TEARING OFF THE STALKS AND LETTING THEM BOIL FOR 1 ½ HOURS OR UNTIL TENDER. REMOVE THE SKIN USING RUBBER GLOVES TO AVOID GETTING REDDENED FINGERS. JUST RUB OFF THE SKIN AND THEN CUT THEM INTO SHREDS.

PUT HALF A CUP OF OLIVE OIL AND THE JUICE OF AN ORANGE AND 1 CRUSHED GARLIC CLOVE AND A DESSERT SPOON OF HONEY AND HALF A CHILLIE INTO A FOOD PROCESSER AND MIX FOR 1 MINUTE. SEASON WITH SALT AND PEPPER.

PUT THE SALAD TOGETHER AND THEN POUR OVER THE DRESSING AND THOROUGHLY MIX.

SALMON AND PLAICE ROLL

TAKE SOME SALMON SLICES AND PLAICE FILLETS AND ROLL THEM TOGETHER ON A DIAGONAL SECURING THEM WITH A TOOTH PICK AND PUT IN TO A ROASTING DISH WITH A CUP OF WATER. COVER THEM WITH TIN FOIL AND BAKE THEM IN THE OVEN FOR 20 MINUTES AT 200 CENTIGRADE.

POUR 1 PINT OF DOUBLE CREAM INTO A FRYING PAN AND ADD 3 TEASPOONS OF DIJON MUSTARD AND REDUCE FOR 5 MINUTES THEN SEASON TO TASTE.

SERVE WITH HOMEMADE CHIPS AND PEAS.

FRESH FRUIT BRANDY

PLACE SOME UNSULPHURED APRICOTS IN A SAUCEPAN WITH SOME WATER AND BRANDY AND BRING TO SIMMERING POINT FOR 20 MINUTES. LEAVE TO COOL AND THEN SERVE WITH CREAM.

Lightning Source UK Ltd.
Milton Keynes UK
UKOW01f0855100616

275991UK00001B/33/P